Shakespeare
on
LEADERSHIP

W

hat man dare,
I dare.

MACBETH, ACT III, SCENE 4

Travel the leading edge.

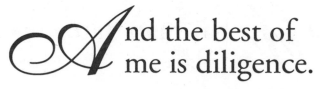

nd the best of
me is diligence.

KING LEAR, ACT I, SCENE 4

Heed the calling of each day.

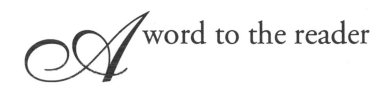word to the reader

For 400 years William Shakespeare's words have been with us, offering essential lessons of the human spirit.

Shakespeare on Leadership began as a search for a precise quote, a robust idea that I needed to convey a point during a talk on leadership. As I made my way through *Hamlet* and *Macbeth* I realized I had rediscovered a timeless treasure that compliments the hundreds of leadership works I have reviewed. I seemed to find the very spirit of leadership on every page.

We quickly formed our *Shakespeare on Leadership* team and shared the joy of rediscovering and chronicling the leadership insight of the Bard.

Here are 150 remarkable excerpts from a broad range of the writer's works. I have added applied leadership commentary, doing my best to compliment the original message. I urge you to apply your own needs, insight and meaning to each entry to best serve your leadership mission.

To scholars, I beg forgiveness for the out-of-context liberties. My goal is to share Shakespeare's messages to generate and promote positive leadership.

And to you, our present and future leaders, I pray these offerings prime your interest in reading the complete works of William Shakespeare. Your spirited quest for wisdom will be justly rewarded.

Shakespeare
on
LEADERSHIP

TIMELESS WISDOM FOR
DAILY CHALLENGES

Frederick Talbott

THOMAS NELSON PUBLISHERS
Nashville • Atlanta • London • Vancouver

Published in Nashville, Tennessee, by Thomas Nelson, Inc., Publishers, and distributed in Canada by Word Communications, Ltd., Richmond, British Columbia, and in the United Kingdom by Word (UK), Ltd., Milton Keynes, England.

Library of Congress Cataloging-in-Publication Data

Talbott, Frederick.
    Shakespeare on leadership / Frederick Talbott.
       p.   cm.
    ISBN 0-7852-7983-0 (pb)
    1. Shakespeare, William, 1564–1616—Quotations. 2. Leadership—Quotations, maxims, etc. 3. Quotations, English. 4. Leadership. I. Title.
PR2892.T35 1994
822.3'3—dc20
                                                 94-11160
                                                   CIP

Printed in the United States of America
1 2 3 4 5 6 7 - 00 99 98 97 96 95 94

*

Acknowledgments

I want to say very special thanks to the *Shakespeare on Leadership* research team:

Patsy Moore-Talbott is an educator, writer, corporate consultant and trainer specializing in career development and human resource issues.

Edith Andrews Talbott is a dedicated reader, scholar, and editor. She has long advocated the application of hope and goodness in effective applied leadership.

W. Keith Shannon is an attorney, management and news media relations consultant and trainer, speaker, and broadcast journalist.

And I thank William Shakespeare. May his words offer refuge and inspiration.

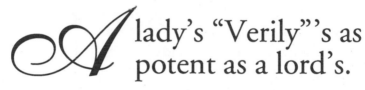

lady's "Verily"'s as
potent as a lord's.

THE WINTER'S TALE, ACT I, SCENE 2

Judge character and ability, not gender.

*S*weet flowers are
slow and weeds
make haste.

RICHARD III, ACT II, SCENE 4

Accept the measured pace of quality.

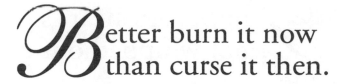

Better burn it now than curse it then.

THE WINTER'S TALE, ACT II, SCENE 3

Handle challenges now, not later.

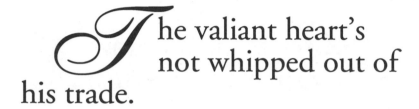

*T*he valiant heart's not whipped out of his trade.

MEASURE FOR MEASURE, ACT II, SCENE 1

Examine your setbacks and refocus.
Then get on with it.

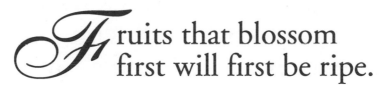

Fruits that blossom
first will first be ripe.

OTHELLO, ACT II, SCENE 3

First to market, first to serve.

*W*hat you have said I will consider. What you have to say I will with patience hear, and find a time both meet to hear and answer such high things.

JULIUS CAESAR, ACT I, SCENE 2

Generate meaningful discussion.

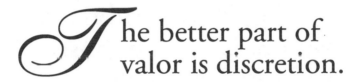

The better part of
valor is discretion.

HENRY IV, 1, ACT V, SCENE 4

Be selective in choice and messaging.

To be generous,
guiltless, and of free
disposition, is to take those
things for bird bolts that you
deem cannon bullets.

TWELFTH NIGHT, ACT I, SCENE 5

Put things in perspective.

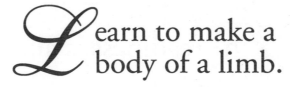

$\mathcal{L}$earn to make a
body of a limb.

RICHARD II, ACT III, SCENE 2

Empower.

The readiness is all.

HAMLET, ACT V, SCENE 2

Live prepared.

*I*f to do were as easy as to know what were good to do, chapels had been churches, and poor men's cottages princes' palaces.

THE MERCHANT OF VENICE, ACT I, SCENE 2

Success unites knowledge and action.

I mean, sir, in delay,
we waste our lights
in vain, like lamps by day.

ROMEO AND JULIET, ACT I, SCENE 4

Treasure — and act on — the moment.

*M*y ventures are not in one bottom trusted, nor to one place, nor is my whole estate upon the fortune of this present year. Therefore my merchandise makes me not sad.

THE MERCHANT OF VENICE, ACT I, SCENE 1

Spread your hopes, plans, and risks. Diversify.

*Y*ou shall command
more with years than
with your weapons.

OTHELLO, ACT I, SCENE 2

The wisdom of experience is formidable.

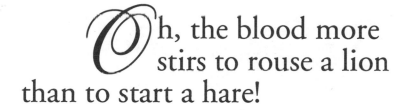

Oh, the blood more
stirs to rouse a lion
than to start a hare!

HENRY IV, 1, ACT I, SCENE 3

Major projects call for major commitment.
And resounding energy.

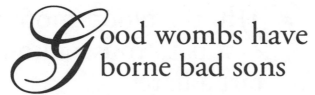

ood wombs have
borne bad sons

THE TEMPEST, ACT I, SCENE 2

Judge the worth—not the name—of products,
acts and services.

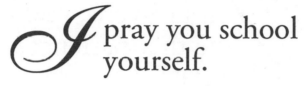

I pray you school
yourself.

MACBETH, ACT IV, SCENE 2

Learn constantly.

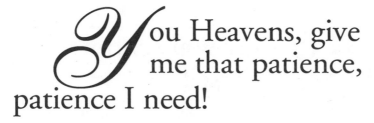

$\mathcal{Y}$ou Heavens, give
me that patience,
patience I need!

KING LEAR, ACT II, SCENE 4

Summon the dedication of endurance.

O

h, it is excellent to have a giant's strength, but it is tyrannous to use it like a giant.

MEASURE FOR MEASURE, ACT II, SCENE 2

Let wisdom gauge your power's range.

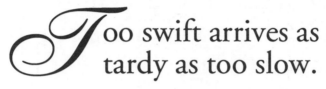

oo swift arrives as tardy as too slow.

ROMEO AND JULIET, ACT II, SCENE 6

Timing is critical. And essential.

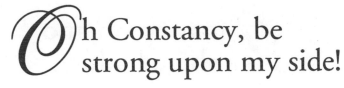

Oh Constancy, be strong upon my side!

JULIUS CAESAR, ACT II, SCENE 4

Apply consistent effort to your tests.

I may command
where I adore.

TWELFTH NIGHT, ACT II, SCENE 5

We lead most comfortably
that which we most cherish.

$\mathcal{L}$ions make
leopards tame.

RICHARD II, ACT I, SCENE 1

Command.

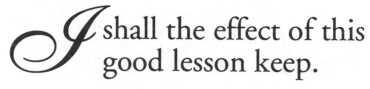

I shall the effect of this
good lesson keep.

HAMLET, ACT I, SCENE 3

Learn from your achievements and your follies.

*T*he truth you speak doth lack some gentleness, and time to speak it in. You rub the sore when you should bring the plaster.

THE TEMPEST, ACT II, SCENE 1

Work to mend, not irritate.

*L*et us be beaten if we cannot fight.

MACBETH, ACT V, SCENE 6

Strengthen every team fibre.

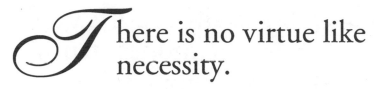

There is no virtue like
necessity.

RICHARD II, ACT I, SCENE 3

Meet needs now.

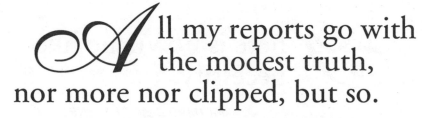

All my reports go with
the modest truth,
nor more nor clipped, but so.

KING LEAR, ACT IV, SCENE 7

Strict accuracy is the safest booster.

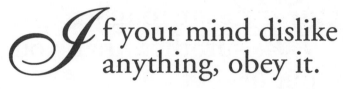

*I*f your mind dislike anything, obey it.

HAMLET, ACT V, SCENE 2

Go with your gut, your knowledge, and your instinct.

We are tougher, brother, than you can put us to 't.

THE WINTER'S TALE, ACT I, SCENE 2

Project your strength.

*K*eep up your bright swords, for the dew will rust them.

OTHELLO, ACT I, SCENE 2

Be ready, and well maintained.

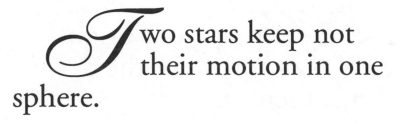

*T*wo stars keep not their motion in one sphere.

HENRY IV, 1, ACT V, SCENE 4

Balance your projects and goals.

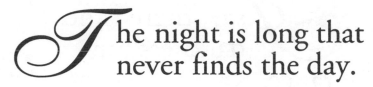

he night is long that
never finds the day.

MACBETH, ACT IV, SCENE 3

Enjoy the light of your lifetime.

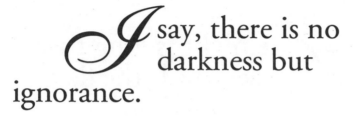

I say, there is no
darkness but
ignorance.

TWELFTH NIGHT, ACT IV, SCENE 2

Learn forever.

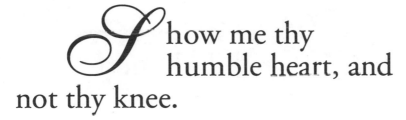

how me thy
humble heart, and
not thy knee.

RICHARD II, ACT II, SCENE 3

Motivate with care.

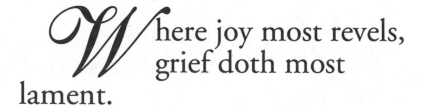

*W*here joy most revels, grief doth most lament.

HAMLET, ACT III, SCENE 2

Create a positive workplace.

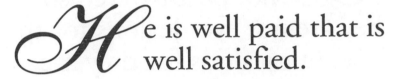

*H*e is well paid that is well satisfied.

THE MERCHANT OF VENICE,
ACT IV, SCENE 1

A joyful profession reaps the best rewards.

*B*ut jealous souls will not be answered so. They are not ever jealous for the cause, but jealous for they are jealous. 'Tis a monster begot upon itself, born on itself.

OTHELLO, ACT III, SCENE 4

Jealousy diffuses teaming.

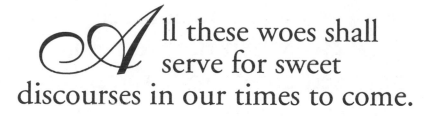

All these woes shall serve for sweet discourses in our times to come.

ROMEO AND JULIET, ACT III, SCENE 5

Even our toughest ordeals may provide rich and lasting memories.

We are not ourselves
when nature being
oppressed commands the mind
to suffer with the body.

KING LEAR, ACT II, SCENE 4

Illness often alters our perspective.

$\mathcal{B}$e merry, gentle. . . . Lift up your countenance, as it were the day of celebration.

THE WINTER'S TALE, ACT IV, SCENE 4

Project positive leadership and standing.

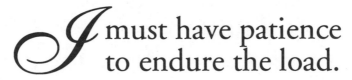

I must have patience
to endure the load.

RICHARD III, ACT III, SCENE 7

View the full dimension of your path. Persevere.

*W*hy, what a wasp-
stung and impatient
fool art thou . . . tying thine ear
to no tongue but thine own!

HENRY IV,1, ACT I, SCENE 3

Listen to others. And learn.

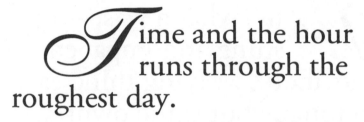

*T*ime and the hour runs through the roughest day.

MACBETH, ACT I, SCENE 3

Be patient that all will pass.

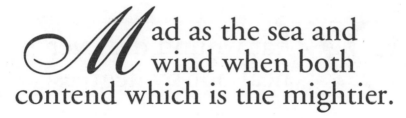

*M*ad as the sea and wind when both contend which is the mightier.

HAMLET, ACT IV, SCENE 1

Avoid unwarranted competition.

What wound did ever heal but by degrees?

OTHELLO, ACT II, SCENE 3

Spurn the quick fix.

$\mathcal{B}$e not lost so poorly in your thoughts.

MACBETH, ACT II, SCENE 2

Organize. Enjoy the adventure of ideas.

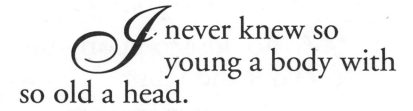

I never knew so
   young a body with
so old a head.

THE MERCHANT OF VENICE, ACT IV, SCENE 1

Constantly learn and reconsider.

$\mathcal{S}$tand, and unfold yourself.

HAMLET, ACT I, SCENE 1

Be open, honest, and forthright.

Be merry, for our time of stay is short.

RICHARD II, ACT II, SCENE 1

Find and share the joy in each day.

W

eigh'st thy words
before thou givest
them breath.

OTHELLO, ACT II, SCENE 3

Consider, then communicate.

*Y*ou'd be so lean that blasts of January would blow you through and through.

THE WINTER'S TALE, ACT IV, SCENE 4

Fortify.

*B*eware of entrance to a quarrel, but being in, bear 't that the opposèd may beware of thee.

HAMLET, ACT I, SCENE 3

Avoid wasteful conflict.
Choose—and win—your fights well.

Who can be wise,
       amazed, temperate
and furious, loyal and neutral,
in a moment? No man.

MACBETH, ACT II, SCENE 3

Know the way of moods
and the flow of human nature.

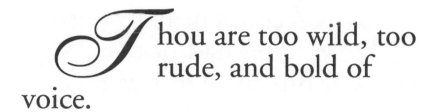

Thou are too wild, too rude, and bold of voice.

THE MERCHANT OF VENICE, ACT II, SCENE 2

Refine.

I could heartily wish
this had not
befallen. But since it is as it is,
mend it for your own good.

OTHELLO, ACT II, SCENE 3

Make the best of the situation.

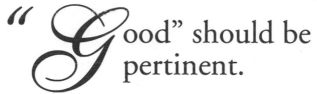

"*G*ood" should be pertinent.

THE WINTER'S TALE, ACT I, SCENE 2

Goodness is essential in your choices.

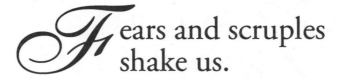

*F*ears and scruples
shake us.

MACBETH, ACT II, SCENE 3

There's always doubt in risks that really matter.

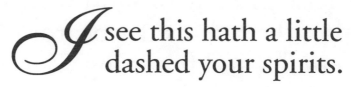

I see this hath a little dashed your spirits.

OTHELLO, ACT III, SCENE 3

Recognize impact and influences.
Respect—and regulate—your reactions.

*H*ow many cowards whose hearts are all as false as stairs of sand wear yet upon their chins the beards of Hercules and frowning Mars, who, inward searched, have livers white as milk.

THE MERCHANT OF VENICE, ACT III, SCENE 2

Test the mettle.

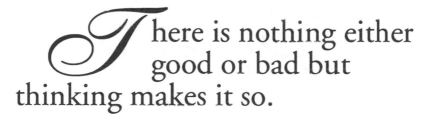

here is nothing either
good or bad but
thinking makes it so.

HAMLET, ACT II, SCENE 2

Live the power of transforming thought.
See the positive and the possible.

B e valiant and live!

RICHARD II, ACT I, SCENE 3

. . . With abandon, courage and faith.

*S*mooth every passion
that in the natures
of their lords rebel.

KING LEAR, ACT II, SCENE 2

Command your emotional posture.

What wisdom stirs amongst you?

THE WINTER'S TALE, ACT II, SCENE 1

Listen to your team.

eaven will
direct it.

HAMLET, ACT I, SCENE 4

Live your faith.

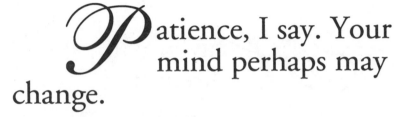

*P*atience, I say. Your
mind perhaps may
change.

OTHELLO, ACT III, SCENE 3

Give decisions time.

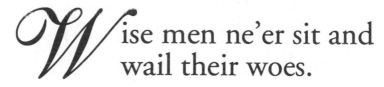

Wise men ne'er sit and wail their woes.

RICHARD III, ACT III, SCENE 2

Action, not words, transcends adversity.

*H*is reasons are as two grains of wheat hid in two bushels of chaff. You shall seek all day ere you find them, and when you have them, they are not worth the search.

THE MERCHANT OF VENICE, ACT I, SCENE 1

Tend to worthy matters.

*T*here are no tricks in plain and simple faith. But hollow men, like horses hot at hand, make gallant show and promise of their mettle, but when they should endure the bloody spur, they fall their crests and like deceitful jades sink in the trial.

JULIUS CAESAR, ACT IV, SCENE 2

Seek courageous associates.

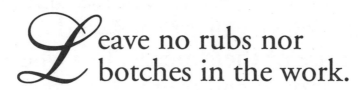

*L*eave no rubs nor
botches in the work.

MACBETH, ACT III, SCENE 1

Excellence promotes exactitude.

B id the honest man mend himself: if he mend, he is no longer dishonest; if he cannot, let the butcher mend him.

TWELFTH NIGHT, ACT I, SCENE 5

Correct your ways and actions or
they will be corrected for you.

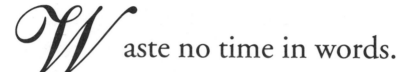

Waste no time in words.

THE MERCHANT OF VENICE,
ACT III, SCENE 4

Get to the point.

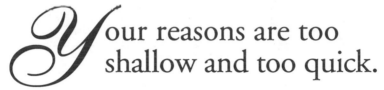

$\mathcal{Y}$our reasons are too shallow and too quick.

RICHARD III, ACT IV, SCENE 4

Think through your decisions. Haste breeds folly.

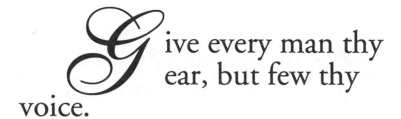

$\mathcal{G}$ive every man thy
ear, but few thy
voice.

HAMLET, ACT I, SCENE 3

Listen.

W

When I have plucked the rose, I cannot give it vital growth again.

OTHELLO, ACT V, SCENE 2

Select your endings carefully, and understand their meaning.

*M*admen have no ears.

ROMEO AND JULIET,
ACT III, SCENE 3

Beware of those who do not listen.

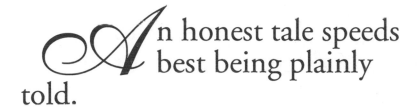

*A*n honest tale speeds best being plainly told.

RICHARD III, ACT IV, SCENE 4

Speak and write clearly. Know truth as the ultimate fortress, and the foundation of trust.

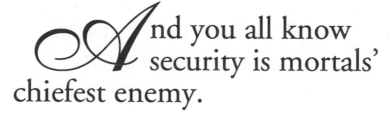

*A*nd you all know
security is mortals'
chiefest enemy.

MACBETH, ACT III, SCENE 5

Welcome worthy risks.

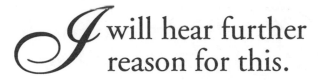

I will hear further reason for this.

OTHELLO, ACT IV, SCENE 2

Investigate.

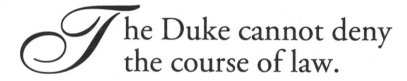

$\mathscr{T}$he Duke cannot deny
the course of law.

THE MERCHANT OF VENICE,
ACT III, SCENE 3

Never overestimate your power.

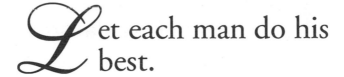

$\mathscr{L}$et each man do his
best.

HENRY IV, 1, ACT V, SCENE 2

Empower your team to excellence.

One good deed dying tongueless slaughters a thousand waiting upon that. Our praises are our wages.

THE WINTER'S TALE, ACT 1, SCENE 2

Rejoice in others' achievements.

I f you dare fight today, come to the field; if not, when you have stomachs.

JULIUS CAESAR, ACT V, SCENE 1

March when you are ready.

*T*he crow doth sing as sweetly as the lark when neither is attended, and I think the nightingale if she should sing by day, when every goose is cackling, would be thought no better a musician than the wren. How many things by season seasoned are to their right praise and true perfection!

THE MERCHANT OF VENICE, ACT V, SCENE 1

Avoid the flock. Find your special voice and timing.

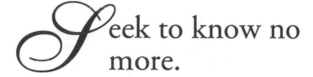

*S*eek to know no more.

MACBETH, ACT IV, SCENE 1

Don't overresearch. Act when you are ready.

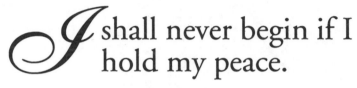

I shall never begin if I hold my peace.

TWELFTH NIGHT, ACT II, SCENE 3

Take the first step, nobly. Initiate.

*I*f you raise this house against this house, it will the woefulest division prove that ever fell upon this cursèd earth.

RICHARD II, ACT IV, SCENE 1

Dispel internal competition. Inspire team excellence.

*T*ake each man's censure, but reserve thy judgment.

HAMLET, ACT I, SCENE 3

Welcome and weigh criticism.
Think through your judgment calls.

*F*or gnarling sorrow hath less power to bite the man that mocks at it and sets it light.

RICHARD II, ACT I, SCENE 3

Recognize and master the power of humor.

*Y*ou have the grace of God, sir, and he hath enough.

THE MERCHANT OF VENICE,
ACT II, SCENE 2

Believe. Your faith will be sufficient.

Shakespeare ON LEADERSHIP

he Devil can cite Scripture for his purpose.

THE MERCHANT OF VENICE,
ACT I, SCENE 3

Recognize the voice of false opinion.

To be tender-minded
does not become a
sword.

KING LEAR, ACT V, SCENE 3

Be fair and firm in counsel, a lion in the fray.

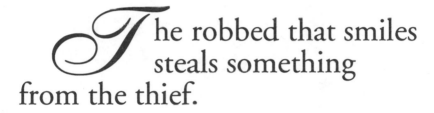

he robbed that smiles
steals something
from the thief.

OTHELLO, ACT I, SCENE 3

Show honor and spirit amid crisis.

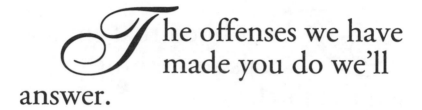

The offenses we have made you do we'll answer.

THE WINTER'S TALE, ACT I, SCENE 3

Responsibility trails a long leash.

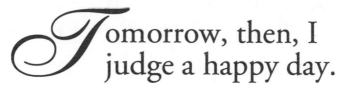

$\mathcal{T}$omorrow, then, I
judge a happy day.

RICHARD III, ACT III, SCENE 4

Look forward to good fortune.

To mourn a mischief
      that is past and gone
is the next way to draw new
mischief on.

OTHELLO, ACT I, SCENE 3

The past is past. Go on now.

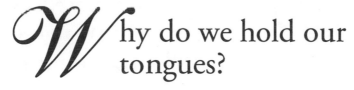

$\mathcal{W}$hy do we hold our tongues?

MACBETH, ACT II, SCENE 3

Silence cements errors.

I dare draw as soon as another man, if I see occasion in a good quarrel and the law is on my side.

ROMEO AND JULIET, ACT II, SCENE 4

Enter the fray when the cause
is both warranted and just.

*O*ur doubts are traitors, and make us lose the good we oft might win by fearing to attempt.

MEASURE FOR MEASURE, ACT I, SCENE 4

Buck fear. Move forward with faith.

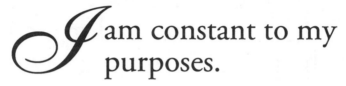

J am constant to my purposes.

HAMLET, ACT V, SCENE 2

Stay the course. Hang in there.

*T*hat sir which serves
and seeks for gain,
and follows but for form, will
pack when it begins to rain, and
leave thee in the storm.

KING LEAR, ACT II, SCENE 4

Recognize and appreciate loyalty.

*S*uit the action to the word, the word to the action.

HAMLET, ACT III, SCENE 2

Share accurate perspective.

*I*t is something of my
negligence, nothing
of my purpose.

TWELFTH NIGHT, ACT III, SCENE 4

We all endure the lessons of mistakes.

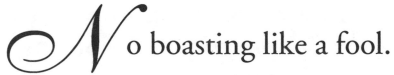

No boasting like a fool.

MACBETH, ACT IV, SCENE 1

Share the truth of your way.
Leave bragging to the insecure.

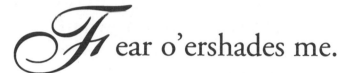

Fear o'ershades me.

THE WINTER'S TALE,
ACT I, SCENE 2

Pierce doubt's shadow with action.

*I*f ever I were willful-negligent, it was my folly. If industriously I played the fool, it was my negligence, not weighing well the end. If ever fearful to do a thing where I the issue doubted, whereof the execution did cry out against the non-performance, 'twas a fear which oft infects the wisest. These, my lord, are such allowed infirmities that honesty is never free of.

THE WINTER'S TALE, ACT, I, SCENE 2

Delay and fear may lead to indecision.

*Y*ou take my house
when you do take the
prop that doth sustain my
house. You take my life when
you do take the means whereby
I live.

THE MERCHANT OF VENICE, ACT IV, SCENE 1

Respect the process of livelihood.

$\mathcal{S}$peak terms of manage to thy bounding steed, Cry "Courage! To the field!"

HENRY IV, 1, ACT II, SCENE 3

Lead your people. And your way.

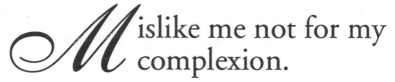

*M*islike me not for my complexion.

THE MERCHANT OF VENICE,
ACT II, SCENE 1

Character and performance are the measures.

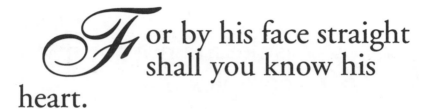

*F*or by his face straight shall you know his heart.

RICHARD III, ACT III, SCENE 4

Our eyes and expressions often reveal our thoughts.

${\cal S}$peak what we feel, not what we ought to say.

KING LEAR, ACT V, SCENE 3

Avoid the paralysis of propriety.
Lead with mind and tongue.

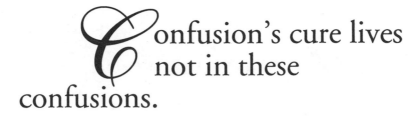

*C*onfusion's cure lives not in these confusions.

ROMEO AND JULIET, ACT IV, SCENE 5

Step away for a clearer view.

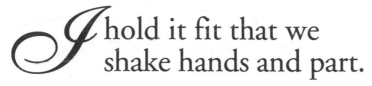

I hold it fit that we
shake hands and part.

HAMLET, ACT I, SCENE 5

Burnt bridges and carried grudges burden the soul
and serve no one well.

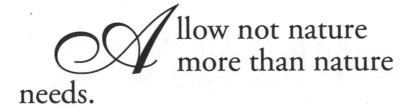

llow not nature
more than nature
needs.

KING LEAR, ACT II, SCENE 4

Be efficient.

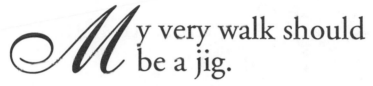

*M*y very walk should be a jig.

TWELFTH NIGHT, ACT 1, SCENE 3

Share your joy of life.

Shakespeare ON LEADERSHIP

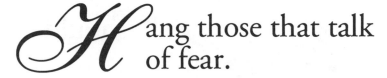

Hang those that talk of fear.

MACBETH, ACT V, SCENE 3

Envision victory. And success.

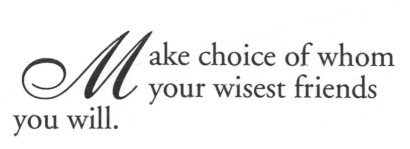

$\mathcal{M}$ ake choice of whom your wisest friends you will.

HAMLET, ACT IV, SCENE 5

Share your trust with those you most respect.

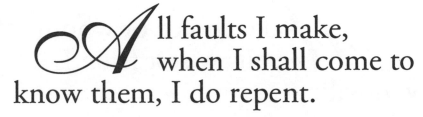

All faults I make,
  when I shall come to
know them, I do repent.

THE WINTER'S TALE, ACT III, SCENE 2

Apologize. And mean it.

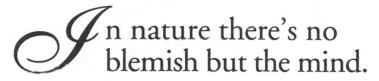

*I*n nature there's no blemish but the mind.

TWELFTH NIGHT, ACT III, SCENE 4

Observe and reason accurately.

O Time, thou must untangle this, not I! It is too hard a knot for me to untie!

TWELFTH NIGHT, ACT II, SCENE 2

Some things have to run their course.

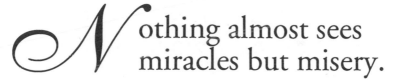*N*othing almost sees miracles but misery.

KING LEAR, ACT II, SCENE 2

The highest hurdle gives the longest view.

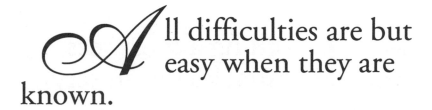

*A*ll difficulties are but easy when they are known.

MEASURE FOR MEASURE, ACT IV, SCENE 2

Knowledge shreds the veil of most confusion.

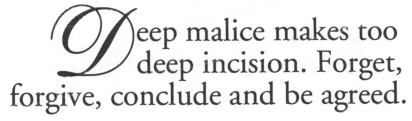

eep malice makes too deep incision. Forget, forgive, conclude and be agreed.

RICHARD II, ACT I, SCENE 1

Move on without the baggage of resentment.

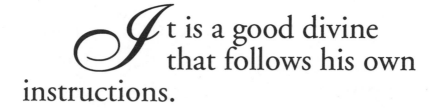

It is a good divine
that follows his own
instructions.

THE MERCHANT OF VENICE, ACT I, SCENE 2

Do as you say.

*C*owards die many
    times before their
deaths, the valiant never taste of
death but once.

JULIUS CAESAR, ACT II, SCENE 2

Live bravely.

What my tongue speaks my right drawn sword may prove.

RICHARD II, ACT I, SCENE 1

Stand for your beliefs.

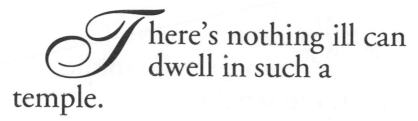

*T*here's nothing ill can dwell in such a temple.

THE TEMPEST, ACT I, SCENE 2

Create a model organization and team.

*Y*ou may relish him
more in the soldier
than in the scholar.

OTHELLO, ACT II, SCENE 1

Know and deploy your people's greatest strengths.

*T*hat light we see is burning in my hall. How far that little candle throws his beams! So shines a good deed in a naughty world.

THE MERCHANT OF VENICE, ACT V, SCENE 1

Light the horizon.

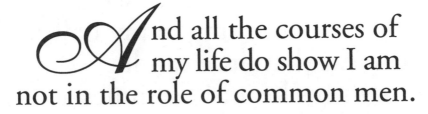

nd all the courses of
my life do show I am
not in the role of common men.

HENRY IV, 1, ACT III, SCENE 1

Be different.

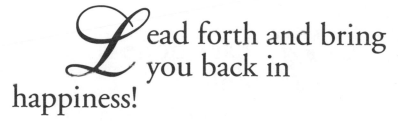

*L*ead forth and bring you back in happiness!

MEASURE FOR MEASURE, ACT I, SCENE 1

Create a joyful venture.

What's done is done.

MACBETH, ACT III, SCENE 2

Learn from the past . . . and then leave it.

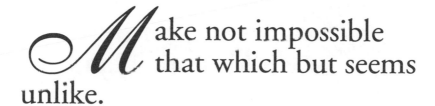

*M*ake not impossible
that which but seems
unlike.

MEASURE FOR MEASURE, ACT V, SCENE 1

Assess your challenges accurately.

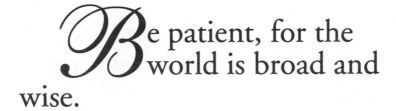

*B*e patient, for the world is broad and wise.

ROMEO AND JULIET, ACT III, SCENE 3

Patience yields the light of understanding.

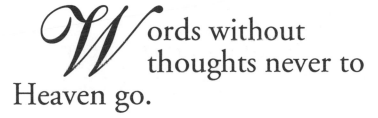

W ords without
thoughts never to
Heaven go.

HAMLET, ACT III, SCENE 3

Communicate with meaning.

N
othing that can be can come between me and the full prospect of my hopes.

TWELFTH NIGHT, ACT III, SCENE 4

Believe, and act accordingly.

*S*crew your courage to
the sticking-place
and we'll not fail.

MACBETH, ACT I, SCENE 7

Live your courage.

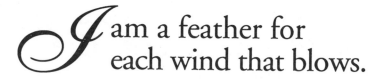

I am a feather for
each wind that blows.

THE WINTER'S TALE,
ACT II, SCENE 3

Be attuned to trends and changes.

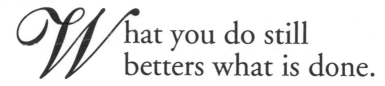

What you do still betters what is done.

THE WINTER'S TALE,
ACT IV, SCENE 4

Your contributions are essential.

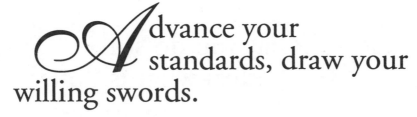

*A*dvance your standards, draw your willing swords.

RICHARD III, ACT V, SCENE 3

Set forth and uphold your values.

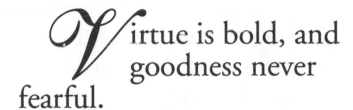

*V*irtue is bold, and goodness never fearful.

*MEASURE FOR MEASURE,
ACT III, SCENE 1*

The truest cause will spark sufficient courage.

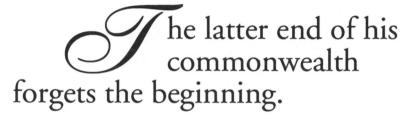

*T*he latter end of his
commonwealth
forgets the beginning.

THE TEMPEST, ACT II, SCENE 1

Recall your original goals and standards.

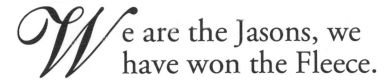

e are the Jasons, we
have won the Fleece.

*THE MERCHANT OF VENICE,
ACT III, SCENE 2*

Champion!

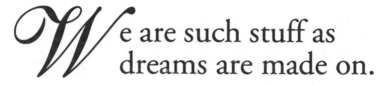

We are such stuff as dreams are made on.

THE TEMPEST, ACT IV, SCENE 1

Confidence is the character of success.

*T*his above all: To thine own self be true, and it must follow, as the night the day, thou canst not then be false to any man.

HAMLET, ACT I, SCENE 3

Live your highest values. Always.

The quality of mercy is not strained, it droppeth as the gentle rain from heaven upon the place beneath. It is twice blest; it blesseth him that gives and him that takes. 'Tis mightiest in the mightiest. It becomes the thronèd monarch better than his crown. His scepter shows the force of temporal power, the attribute to awe and majesty wherein doth sit the dread and fear of kings. But mercy is above this sceptered sway, it is enthronèd in the hearts of kings, it is an attribute to God himself, and earthly power doth then show likest God's when mercy seasons justice.

THE MERCHANT OF VENICE, ACT IV, SCENE 1

Mercy is a measure of leadership.

What I can do I will.

OTHELLO, ACT III, SCENE 4

Act. Perform.

A good leg will fall, a straight back will stoop, a black beard will turn white, a curled pate will grow bald, a fair face will wither, a full eye will wax hollow. But a good heart . . . is the sun and moon . . . for it shines bright and never changes, but keeps its course truly.

HENRY V, ACT V, SCENE 2

Go in goodness, and let goodness be your cause.

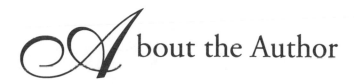 bout the Author

Frederick Talbott is a professional communications educator, journalist, attorney and speaker who has shared his Positive Leadership message with thousands of public and private sector professionals. He is founder of Talbott Communications, which specializes in leadership communications, public and news media relations and career development counseling and services. A native of Virginia, he has taught at Midlands Technical College and Old Dominion University, and is currently Professor for the Practice of Management at Vanderbilt University's Owen Graduate School of Management. He resides in Franklin, Tennessee.